INTERROBANG

PREVIOUS *To the Lighthouse*
POETRY PUBLICATION PRIZE WINNERS

2010: *Spoke & Dark* by Carolyn Guinzio

2009: *In the ice house* by Genevieve Kaplan

ZZ	SINGLE Mo	S

Customer:
Carlos Perez

L WED AM

Interrobang

Piazza, Jessica

4E-06-02-A3

W3-BJZ-845

No CD

Used - Very Good

9781597097222

Picker Notes:
M _____ 2 _____
WT _____ 2 _____
CC _____

70112345

[Amazon] Oregon Trail Book Company: 114-1469526-2160214

1 Item

1070476447

Reno Monday Singles Queue

Ship. Created: 1/31/2020 10:17:00 PM
Date Ordered: 2/1/2020 12:10:00 AM

INTERROBANG

POEMS

JESSICA PIAZZA

RED HEN PRESS | *Pasadena, CA*

Book design and layout by Aly Owen
Cover design by Rebecca Buhler

Library of Congress Cataloging-in-Publication Data
Piazza, Jessica, 1977–
  [Poems. Selections]
  Interrobang : poems / Jessica Piazza.—First edition.
    pages cm
  ISBN 978-1-59709-722-2
  1. Sonnets, American. I. Title.
  PS3616.I213I58 2013 811'.6—dc23
                        2012042831
The Los Angeles County Arts Commission, the National Endowment for the Arts,
the City of Pasadena Cultural Affairs Division, Sony Pictures Entertainment, the Los
Angeles Department of Cultural Affairs, and the Dwight Stuart Youth Fund partially
support Red Hen Press.

The publication of this book was made possible by A Room of Her Own Foundation's
To the Lighthouse Poetry Publication Prize, awarded in 2011 for the best unpublished
poetry collection by a woman. The 2011 prize is sponsored through the generosity of
Vickie Giblin.

First Edition
Published by Red Hen Press
www.redhen.org

Acknowledgments

I'll start with heartfelt thanks to A Room of Her Own Foundation for all the important work they do for women writers, to Red Hen Press for supporting that work, to Vickie Giblin for generously making it possible, and to Eloise Klein Healy, for honoring this book with the *To the Lighthouse* Poetry Publication Prize.

I'm also grateful to the following venues for publishing poems from this collection, whole or in part: *42 Opus, Anti-, Barefoot Muse, Barrelhouse, Chaparral, Coconut, Connotation Press: Congeries, Country Dog Review, di-verse-city, If, Indiana Review, La Fovea, Mid-American Review, The Missouri Review, National Poetry Review, The New Orleans Review, No Tell Motel, Ocho, The Offending Adam, Pebble Lake Review, Rattle, TheThe,* and *Women's Conversation Quarterly.*

Otherwise, whatever is good or terrible in this book is only partially my fault. The rest of the responsibility goes to the following wonderful people:

Jill Alexander Essbaum, for being my soul sister and poetic other half. Winnie Lee, for a lifetime of inspiration and tough love. Rebecca Lindenberg, for always offering a safe sounding board in a storm (and tolerating mixed metaphors like that). Heather Aimee O'Neill, for fifteen years and counting of advice and encouragement. Joshua "Crash" Rivkin, who keeps it real for me, in poetry and life. Eric McHenry, who got this party started. Meaghan McKee for dragging me through the crazy.

My mother Ellen and my sister Lisa, for everything. The Piazzas, who have loved me so well. The Kranes, my brothers. The Flying Jaroszewicz Family, for their love and Sunday dinners. For everyone gone, but especially: Mildred and David Krane, the Lennards, Craig Arnold, Dave Piekos, and, of course, my father, Salvatore Richard

Piazza, who would be proud that his "professional student" finally kept her eye on the prize. I miss you all.

Professors Carol Muske-Dukes, David St. John, Susan McCabe, Aimee Bender, Dana Johnson, Michael Walsh, Kurt Heinzelman and Michael Adams, who helped shape my writing. Tom Cable, both an amazing scholar of prosody and an amazing person; I continue to wish you were my uncle. David Lehman and Stacey Harwood, who are true friends in this crazy po-business world. My *Barrelhouse* Boys, for surviving Hurricane Jess. *The Offending Adam* gang for letting me hitch a ride.

Hilary, Alexis, Crystal, Courtney, Fong, Danielle, Seth, JH, Terry, KZed, Henry, Gaston: your friendships mean the world to me. Elizabeth, Cody, R.J., Jim, Marc, Vieve, Bree, Paula, Kelli, Janalynn, Josh B., Maggie: your wise council in writing and life means everything.

"Melophobia" is for Al Haney; "Achluophilia" is for Winnie Lee; "Pediophilia" is for Christine Piazza; "The Prolific" exists because Josh Rivkin made me shut up and work; "Thalassophilia" is for Jeffrey, with regrets; "Panophilia's" original dedication was dead wrong; "Apeirophilia" is for Peter Talley and Heather O'Neill; "Nephophobia" is for Maya Zeltser Kaplan.

And of course, *all* of this is for Artur Jaroszewicz. *Wszystko. Kocham cię, Aku.*

For my mother and sister,
whose many fears can't even touch the sheer enormity of their love.

TABLE OF CONTENTS

INTERROBANG

This is the radiant House of Love at the side of the road. This is Selfless Agony of Sweethearts, Holidays, Popular Causes & Songs, History, and all the other forms of compulsion and echo, echo and compulsion. Yes. Oh. Yes. Oh.
—LAURA KASISCHKE

Without obsession, life is nothing.
—JOHN WATERS

Interrobang: a punctuation mark designed for use especially at the end of an exclamatory rhetorical question.
—MERRIAM-WEBSTER, 2012

MELOPHOBIA

Fear of music

They'll tell you there are only two ways: flawed
windpipes that knock like water mains behind

thin walls or else a lovely sound like wood-
winds sanded smooth—no middle ground. They'll find

you practicing your scales, determined not
to fail. A voice too frail, too thin, *begin*

again, again, again, now overwrought,
now under-sung; not done. They recommend:

just sound as much yourself as possible.
But we know *possible* is slippery.

As my New York's an ocean filled with steel,
your Texas is an ocean, too, of sky.

Sing into a conch and you'll sound like yourself.
Sing into a conch and you'll sound like the sea.

People Like Us

Remade again, we make the same mistakes again:
unthinking love like insects lustfully swerving loops.
Like most girls, I stoke mental midnight barbeques—
destroy incriminating artifacts, defend,
absolve the most foregonely inconclusive men.
By day I play nonstop *if/then*, internally pluck
a love me, love me not lament. And when
he goes, I go too far; turn hard. I bolt the locks
behind him, one by one. But always when he comes
I weave a line from gauze, thin thread for him to climb
from her to me once more, decision time
delayed again. He can't be sure. I'm sure I've done
things wrong. But he attracted me; it happened, still.
And now our love's not *whether*, but *how long until*.

It isn't *whether*. No. Only: *how long until*
how bad it gets. So quick, our clutch. Sluggish, our rift.
How costly this, a wished subletting of the heart.
Not mine to squat in; he's not mine (*it's fine*). But still:
that sock-to-the-stomach, sudden hollow *Ugh!* You see
the ante? I'm already *un* and *raveling*;
this scanty hope swan-songing my integrity.
(But maybe, also, just a little, *reveling*?
Piñata pricked, unpilfered? Tamed tsunami swell?
An overflowing loving cup?) Tut, tut! Too cursed.
Too much. I won't allow it. Silly, sad, or worse:
tonight I'll disavow these high jinks, hurts, these hells.
(*I will? I might.*) I must. Such surefire track to lack,
a certain fade to black . . . Oh, fuck it. Holler *back*.

Drawn curtain: faded, black. We fucked. We hollered. Back-
tracked and let sunlight in. Repeated. Weekended
in secret. Got outed. Paused. Rebounded. Tended
belabored hearts, but badly. Madly loved. Attacked
covertly. Wept explicitly. Like sailors pressed
to duty on a ship, we gauged our endless trip
in knots; threw cannonballs of angry *nots*, then stripped
our decks with unexpected *yeses*. Reaped such bless-
ings, only to blaspheme them. Wars, then truces: meant
them. Didn't mean them. Lost him and redeemed him. Pleased
him. Keened. Appeased no one. Repeated. When he ceased
his meanness, I retreated. Wanted, but discounted
what I needed. Didn't know I ended when
this first began. But I would do it all again.

When this began, I knew I'd do it. Fall again,
do wrong again. Born into debt, I know I owe
for every weapon, every word. Each lie, each sin,
each deed a bead that slides along a wire in rows,
internal abacus to tally each offense.
Together, we hurt everything we touch; apart,
ourselves. How do we choose? At some point, counterpoint
is pointless—only voices voicing dissonance.
Our bodies: losing arguments we enter in-
to too relentlessly, astride a fence we see
can't pen us endlessly. We'll pay eventually.
Your stroke, your fingers at my throat, the paraffin
that I become: we are both crime and smoking gun.
And we'll continue hiding it from everyone.

We can't continue hiding. Almost everyone
is hiding; almost everyone is getting caught.
Distraught, we fight. We keep our shutter-eyelids shut
against the doormat-sleeping days we know will come.
And every winsome man's like him—an eyelash shy
of possible. And every frantic woman wants
to get to the heart of a fleeing, wing-beating heart.
People like us: we're dust, we're everywhere. We lie
in spaces between places praying madly for
each other, staying mad at one another, hot
because we're bothered. Chasing careless fathers or
neglectful mothers. Listen well: I love him, but
it's over. The inevitable mess we've been,
unmade again. Mistake I'll never make again.

ASTHENOPHOBIA
Fear of weakness

Hallow

    A holy man holds holly plants aloft,
    so wholly bent on kissing every saint.

    Though he mis-thought (it's mistletoe he wanted),
    my haunted face will dip beneath the branches,

    masquerading as each missing martyr.
    Watch me barter for his hijacked heart.

Hollow

    What wasn't there was never mine to lose.
    (Empty: the promise. Empty: the noose.)

    When he pressed the depression at my throat,
    he was not cruel. I was not forced.

    Like me, the tree's worst weakness is its hollow.
    I always do regret tonight tomorrow.

LILAPSOPHOBIA

Fear of tornadoes and hurricanes

Preparedness: a myth. Imagine it:
two city rivers overflow, converge.
Graffiti-covered handball walls afloat—
new arks—above the subway cars submerged
like sunken ships. Two weeks ago a row
of stubborn Brooklyn brownstones doffed their lids
to twisters, skylighting the high-lit glow
of street lamps bending at the waist from winds.
Undone beneath the raised hand of the bay
my house abuts, one year the water touched
our knees before we fled. But flood's not much
compared with these cyclonic days. No way
to gauge you: wrath or pleasure, unfixed track
away or toward. Untoward, you leave no wake.

CLITHROPHILIA
Love of being enclosed

Like lighter flame in wind, you wind your hand
around the ember of my bending body.
Such wonders, harbored. Undiscovered land
enfolded, but not claimed. Unnamed, I'm hardly
less inclined to burrow in these covers.
But, Lover. Don't hover above me, laughing,
friendly. Instead, end me where you begin:
pressed to the fence of you—then beyond, within.
Such tunnels summon. Crushing fog above
doubly envelopes our shelter of bed.
And I've ached for it all: a closet; a stall;
the crevice between your flesh and the wall.
A way to forsake this freedom I've heeded
too often. Your darkness. This coffin.

Automatonophilia

Love of things that falsely represent a sentient being

You married a marionette for the lumbering way
she succumbs to teeth. You saw; she sways
and says *okay*. And she admires the daze
you move in, hydroplaning days away:
exultant accidents. Instead of me,
a blissful wooden girl; a wooden knee
submitted for exhibit. Deadened trees:
the shelter you inhabit. And didn't we
expect it, eking out animatronic
epochs on the sofa? Both electric—
me with boredom; you ran programs: tricks
for trenchant eyes. Disguised, the lists you ticked
led straight to this. Your love nest: nuts and bolts,
no musts. No lust. No faults, and no one's fault.

ACHLUOPHILIA
Love of darkness

My tired love sleeps. His eyes alive with movement:
flicker, flicker, mimicking trains and halfway
open. Tragic: one should be blind when sleeping;
waking's already

hardship, overload of the heart. Awake, the
body blinks, incredulous: stunned and working.
Mornings waking, swept by the moving world, he
whispers of seeing,

talks of seeing halfway in sleep—the curse of
sleeping sight, the bedfellow shadows, how the
dark is never static the way we dream it
must be. He tells me

we've been here, surviving for hundreds of years, half
dozed. The minutes fly in the day. At night we
watch each other, watching. I sleep. I dream his
dreams of a moving

darkness. In my dreams my own eyes half open,
watching him, asleep, and I see him sleeping,
seeing, moving. Night, when I'm covered with his
eyes, and his eyes won't

cover him. It's night, and I can't distinguish
sleep from sight. I move, and I understand him:
we have lived for years, somewhere in between the
blink and the blindness.

ANABLEPHOBIA

Fear of looking up

White clapboard crosses dot the highway like
so many road signs pointing up, somewhere
impossible to travel to. And more,
a rush of diamond signs appear each mile.
Some read just: *THINK.* Those mark an accident.
Others: *Why Die?* And those mean someone did.
One day I heard a man say that his wife
gave up the ghost. But he was like a ghost.
Maybe that's the truth. We die to leave
the losses that we cannot give away.
We drive too drunk. We drive too close to things.
We die to tempt the edges that we fear.
We die to rise. We die to travel up.

Heresyphilia

Love of radical deviation

The way change sounds you think there'll always be
more of it; jingling cacophony for the bus ride, for the
laundromat, reinventing itself the way change does—
hands empty one moment and the next, windfall. You'd
think all change happens that way: a misinterpreted
conversation and suddenly you're in Rhode Island, two
days later, four hundred miles and gas money you didn't
have, your last quarter plinking into the steel eyeslit of
a vibrating bed the likes of which you've only seen in
movies, highway high-beams bursting two by two in
the window like searchlights, working alchemy on your
parasol of cigarette chain-smoke so the whole damn room
shines like a steel ceiling. The way change happens you'd
think the air always looked like this, like furious fog
hiding the highest peaks of a bridge inside her coat, but
a breeze shivers through the room and now everything's
different, and you're younger than you remembered and
Rhode Island is perfect, perfect. The conversation was
not misinterpreted, you see that now, it was a dozen
conversations plaited together to keep them tidy and
smaller than they were. You left because you wanted to.
There was nowhere to go, but here: the extraordinary thing
about the horizon is that it is everywhere.

ATEPHILIA
Love of ruin

A phantom feeling: lashes fluttering
against my cheek. No flesh, no nerve. Wax wings:
imaginings that spring from wish alone.
The thirsty wanderer endures the same
fateful mirage: eats sand and tastes champagne.
You seem so whole; I'm left no room to mourn
the rubble we've become. The pilgrimage
we make each day; our devastated bed
beguiles. We are the sights to see. Engaged
by graveyard days, I rest against your head-
stone chest like flowers, so you'll understand
what wilting is. One kiss with ravaged lips.
Embrace with wasted lust. Remaindered man
and woman wrecked by wants. This mess is us.

BASIPHILIA
Love of falling

We wake and walk to find an oak that fell
with no one there to hear. Old questions stand.
I press my ear toward ground to feel or not
to feel remainders of the sound it did
or didn't make. My lover laughs. Without
the noise, without the cavalcade that trunk
and branches make collapsing, what is left
for us is only aftermath. He knows
how new a silent, upturned tree must be
for me. He knows that it depresses me:
I'll never know the music its fall might
have made. He reaches for my arm. He pulls
me toward decaying ground. The tender sound
our falling bodies make is small, but sure.

Xenoglossophobia
Fear of foreign languages

The background's Brighton Beach. Acrylic, yes
but her Cyrillic written here is thick
as paint already. This new house—gauze house
of family faintly sketched, smudged pencil, chalk,
ghost house—around the figure is not quite
translucent. Young, the figure sits as though
behind tight curtains. Young, the figure paints
new letters on white walls. The background's cold
and iron hard. The figure, from a book,
is kneeling, gripped by pages, ciphers strange
and riveting. Outside, blank walls. Brown brick.
The unfamiliar signs that seem to change
like hours. The figure of her speech is bright:
gray sea, white house, red slash that is her heart.

KOPOPHOBIA
Fear of fatigue

The pension in Prague had no alarm—
we missed the early train we stayed awake
to catch. My fault, our doomed attempt to sleep
in shifts; I thought I wouldn't doze mine off.
For us, no clear Hungarian lake to see
the sun's eclipse; it shadowed us outside
the train, out-dulled by clouds. We caught our breath
in Budapest. We fell in love—adored
this city, thriving on its brokenness.
The bleak facades of burned-through tenements
were testament to how destruction does
not mean the thing destroyed was beautiful
before. Those dragging weeks we built and razed
each day, and nothing that we made endured.
Our statuary garden songs were frail
as monuments composed of candle wax.
Your sketchbook left on the Bazilka floor
like trash; my notebook sloughing ink in rain.
It was a mess, but we make art that's made
for drowning. On the bridge by the Danube,
that storm deluged the city as we ran,
outpacing it until it caught us, sang
staccato rain into our hair and fled
too frantically ahead. I never said
I loved that broken way you looked when things
went wrong. I should have. And I can't forget
the fire-chewed bricks, the statues saved from riots;
how they braved ruin. We could not survive it.

PHOBOPHILIA
Love of fear

The censors will reveal the body, but
black out the eyes. The art of listening
will be unnecessary. Every stop:
a not-lewd interlude. We pause to catch
our breath: it's trapped. Tomorrow: paradise.
Tomorrow, trucks idling at yellow lights
will dash, will crush the thousand hands that wave
unvoiced applause. And then: mass graves. And time
in estrus. Every life contained and wide
as boulevards. Tomorrow, circuses
will drop the safety mesh, disaster checked
for falling flyers with brute prayer alone.
Though some will slip, we know the system will
be wholly good. It will, if it is willed.

Caligynephobia

Fear of a beautiful woman

I carry who
I used to be
inside my heart,
a sleight of hurt.

The ugly girl
I was at first
lives in this fist,
my hidden trick.

Those nights when hand-
some boys unstick
and exit, quick,
I wake her up

still in my clutch,
enraged. Then: punch.

Aerophobia

Fear of drafts or airborne noxious substances

Clipper of breath, ship-bound, I sail with it.
I let it fill me in. There's nothing here,
without, that harms within. Drink in the draft.
Whistle through my chewed-up pen cap—nearly
fume, almost contaminant: as near
a version of us touching lips we'll share
again. You think it's chilly, friend? Just wait
until the porch breeze rushes through the gate
I've built around the bed. You'll shiver then,
because my shivers ceased. No, I can't foul
your nervous lungs, and no, I'll never own
an arsenal so pathological
it spoils the air. If what you fear is true,
the poison in the atmosphere is you.

PEDIOPHILIA
Love of dolls

The week her daughter died, the room her girl
had occupied became a home for dolls.
The first an angel: fearsome, glass-gazed gift
to dull a mother's utter grief; the next
a paint and porcelain she numbly bought
from QVC. It looked like *her*. And now
she sees her small grandchildren grow, and knows
it's good. But they can't guess each small doll dress
arranged by day comes into disarray
by night. They bring her more, naïve. Don't know
she weeps in the overflowing sea of limbs
that manage, year by year, to commandeer
the bed, the floor, and more. An orphanage
of girls. A thousand eyes that cannot shut.

HIEROPHILIA

Love of sacred things

Pray

Along a fault line—yours, mine, or ours—
the church bells in this earthquake shake.
Off-put, they find autonomy.
Canticle, laud and litany.
Our beauty rouses reveille.
But dampened revelry, tonight,
despite our not-quite incidents.
Elegy, requiem, incant.
Disposed to quaking, cant and chant,
an evensong unsacredly
intoned, incessant as Sunday.
Carol, compline, threnody.
Choral, descant, psalm and lay.
We'd never love that way.

Prey

If we've been trapped beneath each other's eyes.
And if this trap. If this sequestering.
If all your fine ideas were less refined.
If you were mine. If Sundays, holidays.
If noon, if dawn, if I keep you too long
on telephones, I will atone. If bones
and earth can quake without consent, you've lent
yourself, the archway I'll stand under. If
you were thunder I could steal, I'd pay
so dearly. If I tracked you. If you came
too quiet. Or: if riot. Alibis
become important. Try it. If a way
to heaven, hell, my house. Tomorrow. If
this sorrow. If I hunt you, will you?

Pry

I'd rise wrapped in the vise of you.
So rapt, like spinning children track
a fixed point with their eyes. And trapped,
we will be twinned with Siamese
desires. Unholy selves enshrined
by arms and lies, tongue-tied. No sin.
We're children, more than any child:
my alibis and your denial.
Your spine unmarrowed, heart a sieve.
I will not be derivative.
Not even if. No Sunday hunt.
No quake, no fixed. No fixing this.
Love's first thought is separation.
Last, to never let it happen.

The Prolific

The red, the blue, the streak of orange stripe—
they're everywhere; so, too, are sound and scent
and still, if all were still the air would pipe
its tactile breath nonstop like bakeries' bent
street fans wafting out exhaust of bread at us
each morning, as we passed on 23rd.
He'd tell me less is more. I'd say: *I've heard.*
But I'd want more; felt there was more of less
for me those days than more of more. The swirl
of world went on, but at the center of
this narcissistic universe: one girl,
dead-stopped. Red cup. Blue shirt. I moved
my hand through orange streaks of hair—a shift
in space that couldn't rift. My eye bereft.

In space that cannot rift, the eye's bereft
of stimuli. A boy was here, but left
an empty seat. I can't just stare at space
that once was filled and not perceive the trace
of stirring lingering. That boy. We walked
down 23rd a lot, and talked, and smoked
and looked at all there was to see, the *more*
of street urbanity. We walked the floor
of gum coating the ground, built toss by toss;
the buildings that had sacrificed their gloss
to sheets of smog. It calmed me: a world built
of what's beneath it, never done, the silt
foot-pounded down by countless hurried feet.
He couldn't love it. It was not complete.

He couldn't love me—I was not complete
the way his wishful eye completed me,
subtracting toward an ideal sum. I'd see
myself lost part by part: white neck, large feet,
wild hair—erased—a disappearing hand
pressed lightly to transparent collarbones.
He wished for tides, forgot they caused sea stones
to wane and yield. But glass worn down to sand,
if not as beautiful, is also not
as delicate. I couldn't disappear
beneath his blink. Instead I found the spot
on 23rd where, when the sun struck clear
glass buildings, streets appeared to multiply.
Then a thousand of me walked away.

A thousand other men could walk away
from me a thousand times, and yet I'd pay
them hardly any mind. The only one
who matters is the one I left. He's gone
the way a flash of bright light goes: still there
in afterimages, a shadow where
a statue stood. But 23rd Street's full
of immigrants who see this way: the pull
of memory placing a tree where raised
wires ought to be; a river where the paved
roads actually run. And if they can erase
a city with nostalgia's sight—replace
the truth with things they loved—I wonder what
my own imperfect eye could substitute.

My own imperfect eye is destitute
when faced with all there is to see. He'd said:
just close them, then. I said: *I can't*—minute
details I missed would haunt me when I did.
But now I do. I walk down 23rd
Street blind, a movie played on loop
beneath my lids. A vast, prolific world
swells all around me, kaleidoscope
of sound and scent redoubling, but I
know nothing of it, only see in flash-
backs. Empty seat. Raised cup, a grip belied
by see-through hands. Unfinished buildings slashed
by vivid streaks of sun; a city wiped
too clean of reds, of blues, of orange stripes.

THALASSOPHILIA
Love of the sea

The Gulf gulls' chants at dusk all sound alike
to me, but symphonies of secret tones
must prove expressiveness beyond the spike
of elegiac grief I hear. I've known
only another coast, but lyrics hold.
One gull might say: *This short-lived breeze. This day:*
most gray. His brother must intone: *I told*
this pair of pier-posts crumbling: wait. Matte sky
stays stable perching on your two bad feet.
And that is Texas singing in a trill
I know. Unbordered world, far from the weight
of my heat-baked adopted land. It's all
music again, at last beyond the fence
of the inland blue-black grackles' dissonance.

THEOPHOBIA
Fear of God

Unglued from truth one day I almost think:
I must be découpage from scraps of God.
Leftover. Fiend. Created—thread and ink
unstitched and pasted. Stolen from the shroud.
Un-bless this dwelling built without consent.
I never chose this ice floe for my home.
Amass no mass. I am the God I've known:
untaken turns unwrecking what wasn't;
a cricket's ticket punched when I crushed it.
Oh, swear these deeds I can't undo are not
divinity in minor chord! Oh lordy
be. Oh, woe is me. And more importantly:
I choose to worship what I'm chosen by.
If you love everyone, then who am I?

EISOPTROPHILIA
Love of mirrors

Impression pressed upon the glass perfects
even the grossest forgeries. Reject
the sea. Reject the turning tide.
Just below clear water, I reside
as duplication of the lake. Take me
away, another underneath again.
What mirrors cannot ditto isn't sin.

EISOPTROPHOBIA

Fear of mirrors

What mirrors cannot ditto isn't sin
simply performed behind the glass. Within
the frame of windowpane, negated dark.
Those fleeting squares reveal our darkness back.
Aloof, the rain plays taps. Above, the trees
are inimitable. Distinct, thus blessed.
Reflected, I am never at my best.

EREMOPHOBIA

Fear of loneliness or of being oneself

Hi I. Hi me, on this, a birthday. Hi,
internal eye of this year's storm. Hello
you: point without an exclamation. Wave
a single hand, then wave the other, pair
them off. A sacrifice concise as this:
pity your pity today, and let it lie.
An alibi for a scoffing enemy.
Myself, and my most toxic company:
myself. These withered candles leak their wax.
What could these last wet decades turn, and wane.
Picture me, today, as a metronome.
I'm home, away, one way, the next, and strike
each hour, and strike again, a single tone,
one arm, one fist. Alone, exalt, against.

ANKYLOPHOBIA
Fear of the immobility of a joint

Locked here, I'm loch-jawed: a Nessie of
tetanus. Unhook me, unhinge me, this
liquid imprisonment. Taciturn
elbow, mulish talocrural, my
most stubborn joint is submerged in your
tallow. This candle, this window, you
squirm like a minnow, repeat like an
echo, arthritic libido. I'm
caught. I'm unmovable. Abjectly
literal. You? Irresistible
force meeting object, we forge into
junction—one tongue in one groove, and we
fit, and we fit again. Limit my
movement. I'll ease your impediment.

PANOPHILIA
Love of everything

Today this weather's better than itself:
all background clamor, siren song, our schemed
and ill-conceiving strategies. This shelf,
chaotic and precariously leaning
next to your appalling bed, a trove
of wonders hovering over us. But love
itself I never deigned to love; all give
and giving in. So I don't understand
my drunkenness on scribble scrawled above
the mirror in the ladies' room: *You're doomed.*
Ecstatic that it's almost true. And though
I should not love you yet—obliged to slow
and genuflect to sense or self-defense—
because of you, I'll love everything else.

Apodysophilia

Love of undressing

When many veils are pared to one what more
to gain obscured? The dance must end. One spin:
the veil has fallen to the floor. One more:
the centrifuge that I become has pinned
you there. Again, I win. Undone, my clasp
has claws. This sloughing of my clothes breaks laws
that aren't written yet. And now my grasp
is masquerading as embrace because
many a lip twixt cup and slip has tried
to bare my cloth-clad heart. But what I hide
is hidden even more the more I show.
Still, all of this means *yes*. The air's desired
caress; I have no *no*. You're sure you know
me? So, you've guessed. *There's nothing to undress.*

PATROIOPHOBIA
Fear of heredity

She's learned to work her family like a field
of failing grain. A tricky heirloom passed
to her at birth—a crop she neither yields

nor reaps. Her mother, tied to Brooklyn, cast
a wish: a heavy, stone-shaped girl. She threw
so far, such skips, she can't get back. And last

night when she dreamed she did return, she knew
it was a dream; each eyelid twitch still miles
between them. Still, her mother's voice: *But you*

do own this land. And maybe it's denial
how she refuses it, won't bend to claim
a side or plant a flag. It's been awhile

since she's owned anything. Even her name:
her father's. Her face, his. Like him, she's not
inclined to argue over heavy things. Like him,

she takes no pride in sweat, no heed in God.
But while his silences hang thick as clothes
that never dry, she tries to make her body

her own, talks loud, denies his heartbeat rose
to shadow hers with quiet minuets,
deficient spins. He can't share what he knows.

She watches, stays away, wishing they'd weight
their expectations down until they drowned
all hope for her. She'd praise the day they'd set

her free; the day they'd let her let them down;
renounce a family tree for solid ground.

APEIROPHILIA
Love of infinity

Before continuum, define discrete.
Two points or pennies on the edge of things.
Now halve that space. *Things never touch.* As if
we don't collide: my skin, unto, into,
your skin. You say that if we pantomime
shared flesh, it doesn't mean we're whole. *Discrete.*
But we collide; we make tautology
of us. We're what we are because we're what
we are—so where's your tangent? I can be
a line, extend the distance to you, in-
finite; bisect you at a fixed point. I'll
bisect you only if I am the line.
If I'm the line, intending to bisect,
I must be infinite; you must be fixed.

Atomosophobia

Fear of atomic explosions

And what about: *again?* If not *explode,*
then *fracture, blaze.* Or, *leave.* One year I wrote
three hundred sixty five laments. The next
I watched two lamps burn out at once. The wreck
of me sees every city gone. Each night
the train implodes: my own New York set right,
then overturned like bowling pins. My God.
But really: what about *again?* What could,
what if, what next. I may not run so fast
next time—not knowing what I know: a blast
of sky and time, of scientific pap.
I need a nap, a borough in my lap
to stroke to sleep, another year of peace,
a bang, a bigger bang. I need release.

Pharmacophilia
Love of drugs

~ This poppy in the
vase will close, after it blooms.
But her wilting is
more like prosthesis. She's not
there, but feels it; swears she is.

~ Seductive seeds like
beads. One hope, one need, and more.
She covets them; glides
each along the abacus
of her calculating heart.

~ Power to calm and
power to kill. Potted here,
they're wilting. Though no
life strives to decorate the
windowsill, she's tired. She will.

~ Poison camouflaged,
she says. They're red as wind-scoured
skin. Exquisite, she
takes them in. And, merciless,
they rise. They take her with them.

~ Scarlet on beige; bright
red on white. Short-lived shock on
neutral life. Lovely
sprays. All is vague. Imagine
her days: all the same, the same.

NEPHOPHOBIA
Fear of clouds

The woman weeps; her wide eyes slowly grow
translucent, eyelids turning membranous
and fluttery. Those lashes beat like wings.
Her vision feels as overcast, she says,
as her entire unleavened life. Small things
all haunt her: uselessness, the endless throw-
away events that dampen days, the sky's
stark darkening as winter months encroach.
But strange: that same sad girl finds butterflies
in summer, softly steals to where they perch
and smoothly clasps one colored wing. She'd see
her power if she knew the slow command
that wing beats have of winds. A deity;
a woman trapping weather in her hands.

ANTLOPHOBIA

Fear of floods

Is ebb the measure of the flow? She goes,
she lets; she skirts the nervous ocean's salt
and semi-circle frowning, knowing take
then give again, not sure how much that get
is worth in give. Such oceans make a lake
of her own basement every year, below
ground where her mother lives and wades in worn-
out foam flip-flops. That stubborn water won't
pull back, as if it knows her mother's own
sharp knack for asking back exact amounts
she gives. A skill she lacks. And like that flood,
she does not choose her low-laid rooms for rest,
but goes, and goes, and stays. She does not flow
there. No. She ebbs. She ebbs to such excess.

ASYMMETRIPHOBIA
Fear of asymmetrical things

Here's the torment only the warped heart knows:

One side withers.   The other grows.   And grows.

CHIONOPHILIA
Love of snow

Past lengthening days I loathed the draining, dazing winter
light; the whitening waking me each blazing winter.

The ashes of our strange, mislaid chronology remained,
but each insistent day came anyway, not phasing winter.

Our boot-prints decked the snowy portico. Or not our boots,
the ghost of them. Such lingerings of one amazing winter.

Revelers strolled the glowing city's slush and sulfur streets. I
wanted to collapse it all like a theater set: razing winter.

I wasted days crazed with waiting for beginnings. But now no
more unending. No more stunned, steadfast stargazing winters.

Forgetting is divine. Divine: a name unfastened from its handcuffed
history. Forgetting has renamed me and I wake, now praising winter.

Erotophobia
Fear of sexual love

This scene's a sad and difficult duet:
etude of *please, next time, I need.* The night's
impossible and lukewarm, slightly wet
and half as thick as sleep. I reach for you,

intrude, appease. Each time, my need beats night
to knees and me awake and heavy-tongued
and thick. Just half-asleep, I reach for you,
your neck, your hipbone, chest. All chaste. I clasp

my knees. You're not awake or, heavy-hearted,
act it. Lucky fan-stirred air has access
to your neck, your hipbone, chest. I chase the asp
that eats its tail. I've failed again. I'm nailed

to slats. Unlucky, too-stirred air repressed
inside a bottle. Wailing hunger martyr
who still eats despite and, flailing, fails
to fill, to save. Your eyes the gimlet gaze

of bottle glass, mine hungry, waiting, bothered
by an appetite that grows too fast. I'm not
saved, never filled; despise this scarlet crave
for you, for hurry. Worn, but sure as salt.

In appetite, there's only *fast* and *not.*
Impossible, our lukewarm *slightly wet.*
My blue hurry, your torn, voiceless halt:
they keen such sad and difficult duets.

KAKORRHAPHIOPHOBIA
Fear of failure

Derailed, your vantage point is not of stairs
you'll scale, but stars you can't. Wrong turns advance
no grace and no divine. Anywhere
you land feels falsely fine. When you commence,
each errand's a half-empty glass to sip
your water from, to sip your wine. You start
a dialogue with *never done,* a trip,
a wire, a current to defibrillate
your half-stopped heart. Breathing uncaught. Unfailed,
you delve. Another devil is de-veiled.
A doppelgänger born with every task:
the evil twin of its unfinishing.
The harbor, never there, is menacing.
Its ebb, unanswered question asked and asked.

WHAT I HOLD

A glint—an intimation of what gleams.
Just simple incidentals; nothing grand
in pomegranates, Coney Island, reams
of new newspapers hitting dawn-dark stands.
The birds I hear don't sound like opera, not
like flutes or piccolos at play. They sound
like birds. Sometimes the birds are all I've got.
There's nothing grand but wakefulness, the ground
I jump from; nothing but the shining air
which might be a light left on for me. A glow,
though small, intense and worthy of my care.
I pity the fragile, but I still forgo
the sturdy cup and choose the demitasse.
Whatever's in my grip, it's made of glass.

Whatever's in my grip, it's made of glass-
blown promises, assurance that forged skin
will harden, change to something that might pass
for beautiful. But though I know that in-
side every crafted sphere there is just air,
I cannot love the space between the words,
can find no pleasure in the silence there.
And if the point is trusting what's unheard—
how every stop, in time, will yield a sound—
the shape I seek is not one I create.
Thorns twist around themselves to form a crown;
they frame an emptiness we'll consecrate.
Without the skips, the beat would not exist.
My hand grasps nothing and still forms a fist.

My hand grasps nothing and still forms a fist
for me to rest my heart against. There's doubt
in everything but what I own: the trysts
I thought were trusts are minor—they amount
to nothing but a blink over the lifetime of the eye.
When subject fails to add up, there's the sum
of my own fingers, vanities, the way
the body shows me just what's mine: the run
of timid freckles sprinting down an arm,
a clavicle to climb, the bones that hold
my weight despite themselves, despite the harm
I've caused. And every story I've been told
is hidden in my spine, a refugee.
Worry my backbone like a rosary.

Worry. My backbone, like a rosary,
cannot withstand the press of all this faith.
I've wrapped myself around the things I see
so tightly that my stories feel like breath—
beholden to them, I inhale their rich
minutiae desperately, but when I let
them out they have been changed. This is a switch
that stripes my best attempts. I need to get
perspective now, and so, unusual
as it may seem, I'll stop to look outside
these lines; to ask if it is sin to pull
myself away from this, or prayer to ride
the story out. But who will answer me?
I'm not a girl who has epiphanies.

I'm not a girl who has epiphanies,
but once one happened, waiting for a light
to change. An ancient woman raised a weak
gnarled fist to tap my window just as night
advanced. I lowered it. She spoke—a voice
as thick and cumbersome as wool—*my feet,
she said, I can't get home.* I had a choice,
but I said no. And she went down the street,
the queue of cars . . . they all said *no*, and *no*
and *no*. I knew this damage was my own;
I had been taught such fears. I knew. And so?
Perhaps I changed my mind and drove her home.
And maybe to this day that choice still seems
like a hint, a minute's inkling of what gleams.

BIOGRAPHICAL NOTE

Jessica Piazza was born and raised in Brooklyn, New York. She has a B.S. in Journalism from Boston University, an M.A. in Creative Writing from UT Austin, and is a Ph.D. candidate in English Literature and Creative Writing at the University of Southern California. She co-founded *Bat City Review* and *Gold Line Press*, is a contributing editor at *The Offending Adam,* and has blogged for *The Best American Poetry* and *Barrelhouse*. Among other places, her work has appeared in *Agni, Indiana Review, Mid-American Review, National Poetry Review, The Missouri Review, Rattle, Hobart,* and *Forklift, Ohio. Interrobang* is her first collection of poems, and winner of A Room of Her Own Foundation's 2011 *To the Lighthouse* Poetry Prize. Her chapbook, "This is not a sky," is forthcoming from Black Lawrence Press in 2014. You can find her at www.jessicapiazza.com.